Wealth Building Secrets: Strategies for Success for Everyone

Table of Contents

Chapter 1: Understanding Wealth Building 1

    The Importance of Financial Literacy 1

    Setting Financial Goals 3

    The Mindset of Wealth Builders 5

Chapter 2: Creating a Solid Financial Foundation 8

    Managing Debt Effectively 8

    Building an Emergency Fund 11

    Investing in Retirement Accounts 13

Chapter 3: Income Generation Strategies 17

    Diversifying Income Streams 17

    Leveraging Passive Income Opportunities 19

    Negotiating Salary and Benefits 21

Chapter 4: Investment Principles for Wealth Building ... 24

    Understanding Risk Tolerance 24

    Asset Allocation Strategies 26

    Real Estate Investing 28

Chapter 5: Advanced Wealth Building Techniques 31

    Tax Planning Strategies 31

- Estate Planning 33
- Leveraging Financial Advisors 35
- Chapter 6: Maintaining and Growing Wealth 38
- Revisiting and Adjusting Financial Goals 38
- Monitoring and Tracking Financial Progress 40
- Giving Back and Philanthropy 42
- Chapter 7: Overcoming Common Wealth Building Challenges 45
- Dealing with Setbacks and Failures 45
- Overcoming Impulse Spending 47
- Handling Family and Relationship Dynamics 49
- Chapter 8: Wealth Building for Everyone 52
- Strategies for Individuals with Low Income 52
- Wealth Building for Entrepreneurs 54
- Wealth Building for Young Adults 56
- Chapter 9: Conclusion 60
- Recap of Key Wealth Building Principles 60
- Tips for Continued Success 62
- Resources for Further Learning 65

Chapter 1: Understanding Wealth Building

The Importance of Financial Literacy

Financial literacy is a crucial skill that everyone should strive to develop in order to achieve success in wealth building. Understanding how to manage money, make smart investment decisions, and plan for the future are all essential components of financial literacy. Without this knowledge, individuals may struggle to build wealth and secure their financial future.

One of the key reasons why financial literacy is so important is that it empowers individuals to make informed decisions about their money. By understanding concepts such as budgeting, saving, and investing, individuals can take control of their financial situation and make choices that will benefit them in the long run. Without this knowledge, individuals may be more susceptible to making poor financial decisions that could negatively impact their wealth building efforts.

Additionally, financial literacy can help individuals to avoid common financial pitfalls that can derail their wealth building goals. By understanding the risks and rewards associated with various financial opportunities, individuals can make more informed decisions that align with their long-term financial goals. This can help individuals to avoid unnecessary debt, make smarter investment choices, and ultimately build wealth more effectively.

Furthermore, financial literacy can provide individuals with the tools they need to plan for the future and achieve their financial goals. By creating a financial plan that outlines their goals and strategies for achieving them, individuals can set themselves up for long-term success. This can help individuals to build wealth over time and secure their financial future for themselves and their families.

In conclusion, financial literacy is a critical skill that everyone should strive to develop in order to achieve success in wealth building. By understanding how to manage money, make smart investment decisions, and plan for the future, individuals can take control of their financial situation and build wealth over time. By prioritizing financial literacy and making informed decisions about their money, individuals can set themselves up for long-term financial success and achieve their wealth building goals.

Setting Financial Goals

Setting financial goals is an essential step in the journey towards building wealth and achieving financial success. Without clear goals in place, it can be challenging to stay motivated and focused on your financial objectives. By setting specific, measurable, achievable, relevant, and time-bound goals, you can create a roadmap for your financial future and track your progress along the way.

Wealth Building Secrets: Strategies for Success for Everyone

One of the first steps in setting financial goals is to determine what you want to achieve. Do you want to save a certain amount of money for retirement? Pay off your debt? Purchase a home or start a business? By identifying your financial goals, you can begin to develop a plan to help you reach them. It's important to be specific and realistic about what you want to accomplish, as vague or unrealistic goals can be difficult to achieve.

Once you have identified your financial goals, it's essential to create a plan to help you achieve them. This plan should include specific steps you will take to reach your goals, such as saving a certain amount of money each month, reducing your expenses, or investing in assets that will help you grow your wealth. By breaking down your goals into smaller, manageable tasks, you can make progress towards achieving them and stay on track.

In addition to creating a plan, it's crucial to track your progress towards your financial goals regularly. By monitoring your income, expenses, savings, and investments, you can assess how well you are doing in relation to your goals and make adjustments as needed. Tracking your progress can also help you stay motivated and focused on your financial objectives, especially when faced with challenges or setbacks along the way.

Setting financial goals is an integral part of wealth building and financial success. By identifying what you want to achieve, creating a plan, and tracking your progress, you can take control of your financial future and work towards building the wealth and security you desire. Whether you are saving for retirement, paying off debt, or investing in your future, setting financial goals can help you stay focused and motivated on your journey towards financial success.

The Mindset of Wealth Builders

The mindset of wealth builders is crucial to their success in achieving financial freedom and abundance. Wealth builders possess a unique set of beliefs, attitudes, and habits that set them apart from the average person. They have a positive outlook on life and are not afraid to take risks in order to achieve their goals. Wealth builders understand that wealth is not just about money, but also about creating a life of abundance in all areas.

One key mindset of wealth builders is the belief in abundance. They believe that there is more than enough wealth and opportunities to go around for everyone. This mindset allows them to think big and dream even bigger. Wealth builders do not limit themselves by scarcity thinking, but instead embrace the idea that the universe is abundant and there is plenty for everyone to achieve their financial goals.

Another important mindset of wealth builders is the willingness to take calculated risks. Wealth builders understand that in order to achieve great wealth, they must be willing to step outside of their comfort zone and take risks that others may shy away from. They are not afraid to fail, as they see failure as a stepping stone to success. Wealth builders know that every failure brings them one step closer to their ultimate goals.

Wealth builders also have a growth mindset, constantly seeking to improve themselves and learn new skills. They understand that in order to achieve wealth, they must be willing to invest in themselves and their own personal development. Wealth builders are lifelong learners, always seeking new knowledge and opportunities for growth. They understand that in order to stay ahead in the constantly evolving world of wealth building, they must be adaptable and open to change.

In conclusion, the mindset of wealth builders is one of abundance, risk-taking, growth, and continuous learning. By adopting these beliefs and attitudes, anyone can become a successful wealth builder and achieve financial freedom and abundance in their lives. Wealth building is not just about money, but about creating a life of abundance in all areas, and it all starts with the right mindset.

Chapter 2: Creating a Solid Financial Foundation

Managing Debt Effectively

Debt can be a major obstacle to building wealth. Whether you have student loans, credit card debt, or a mortgage, managing your debt effectively is crucial to achieving financial success. In this chapter, we will discuss strategies for managing debt and reducing financial stress.

The first step to managing debt effectively is to create a budget. By tracking your income and expenses, you can identify areas where you can cut back and allocate more money towards paying off debt. This will help you prioritize which debts to pay off first and create a plan to tackle them systematically.

Another important strategy for managing debt is to negotiate with creditors. If you are struggling to make payments, don't be afraid to reach out to your creditors and explain your situation. Many creditors are willing to work with you to come up with a payment plan that fits your budget. By negotiating lower interest rates or extended payment terms, you can make your debt more manageable.

Consolidating your debt can also be a helpful strategy for managing debt effectively. By combining multiple debts into one loan with a lower interest rate, you can streamline your payments and potentially save money on interest. However, it's important to carefully consider the terms of the consolidation loan and make sure it will actually save you money in the long run.

Finally, it's important to avoid taking on new debt while you are working to pay off existing debts. By living within your means and avoiding unnecessary purchases, you can focus on reducing your debt and building wealth for the future. Remember, managing debt effectively is a key component of achieving financial success and building wealth for everyone.

Building an Emergency Fund

Building an emergency fund is a crucial step in achieving financial stability and success. An emergency fund is a pool of money set aside for unexpected expenses such as medical emergencies, car repairs, or job loss. Without an emergency fund, individuals may find themselves in a difficult financial situation when unexpected expenses arise. In this subchapter, we will explore the importance of building an emergency fund and provide practical strategies for creating and maintaining one.

One of the key benefits of having an emergency fund is that it provides a sense of security and peace of mind. Knowing that you have money set aside for unexpected expenses can help alleviate stress and anxiety about potential financial hardships. Additionally, having an emergency fund can help prevent individuals from falling into debt when faced with unexpected expenses. Instead of relying on credit cards or loans to cover expenses, individuals can use their emergency fund to weather financial storms without accumulating debt.

When building an emergency fund, it is important to set realistic savings goals based on your income and expenses. Aim to save at least three to six months' worth of living expenses in your emergency fund. Start by setting aside a small amount of money each month and gradually increase your savings as your financial situation improves. Consider automating your savings by setting up automatic transfers from your checking account to your emergency fund to ensure consistent contributions.

Another important aspect of building an emergency fund is to keep your fund separate from your regular checking or savings account. Consider opening a separate high-yield savings account or money market account specifically for your emergency fund. This will help prevent you from dipping into your fund for non-emergency expenses and ensure that your fund continues to grow over time. Additionally, keeping your emergency fund separate from your regular accounts will make it easier to access in case of an emergency.

In conclusion, building an emergency fund is a critical step in achieving financial security and success. By setting realistic savings goals, automating your savings, and keeping your fund separate from your regular accounts, you can build a strong financial foundation that will help you weather unexpected expenses and avoid falling into debt. Remember, it's never too late to start building your emergency fund – the sooner you start, the sooner you can enjoy the peace of mind that comes with knowing you are financially prepared for whatever life may throw your way.

Investing in Retirement Accounts

Investing in retirement accounts is essential for everyone, regardless of age or income level. Retirement accounts, such as 401(k)s, IRAs, and Roth IRAs, offer tax advantages that can help you save for retirement more effectively. By contributing to these accounts, you are not only preparing for your future but also taking advantage of the power of compound interest.

Wealth Building Secrets: Strategies for Success for Everyone

One of the key benefits of investing in retirement accounts is the tax advantages they offer. Contributions to traditional 401(k)s and IRAs are made with pre-tax dollars, which can lower your taxable income and reduce your tax bill. Additionally, any investment gains within these accounts are tax-deferred, meaning you won't pay taxes on them until you withdraw the money in retirement. Roth IRAs, on the other hand, are funded with after-tax dollars, but withdrawals in retirement are tax- free, making them a valuable tool for tax diversification.

When it comes to investing in retirement accounts, it's important to start early and contribute regularly. By starting to save for retirement as soon as possible, you give your money more time to grow through the power of compound interest. Even small contributions made consistently over time can add up significantly, thanks to the compounding effect. Additionally, many employers offer matching contributions for 401(k) accounts, so be sure to take advantage of this free money by contributing enough to get the full match.

Another benefit of investing in retirement accounts is the ability to diversify your investments. Most retirement accounts offer a wide range of investment options, including stocks, bonds, mutual funds, and ETFs. By spreading your investments across different asset classes, you can reduce your risk and potentially increase your returns over time. It's important to review your investment allocations regularly and adjust them as needed to ensure they align with your risk tolerance and retirement goals.

In conclusion, investing in retirement accounts is a crucial step in building wealth and securing your financial future. By taking advantage of the tax benefits, starting early, contributing regularly, and diversifying your investments, you can set yourself up for a comfortable retirement. Whether you're just starting out in your career or nearing retirement age, it's never too late to begin investing in retirement accounts and taking control of your financial future.

Chapter 3: Income Generation Strategies

Diversifying Income Streams

In order to truly build wealth and secure a stable financial future, it is crucial to diversify your income streams. Relying solely on one source of income leaves you vulnerable to financial instability in the event of job loss or economic downturn. By diversifying your income streams, you can create multiple sources of revenue that can support you in times of need and help you continue to grow your wealth over time.

One way to diversify your income streams is to explore passive income opportunities. Passive income is money earned with little to no ongoing effort, such as rental income from properties, royalties from intellectual property, or dividends from investments. By investing in passive income streams, you can generate additional revenue without having to actively work for it, allowing you to build wealth more efficiently and with less stress.

Wealth Building Secrets: Strategies for Success for Everyone

Another way to diversify your income streams is to explore side hustles or freelance opportunities. In todays gig economy, there are countless ways to earn extra money on the side, whether it's through driving for a ride-sharing service, selling handmade goods online, or offering your skills as a freelancer. By taking on a side hustle, you can increase your income and reduce your reliance on a single source of revenue, giving you more financial security and flexibility.

Investing in the stock market is another way to diversify your income streams and build wealth over time. By purchasing stocks or other securities, you can earn dividends and capital gains that can provide you with additional income and help your wealth grow. While investing in the stock market carries risks, it can also offer significant rewards if done wisely and with a long-term perspective.

Overall, diversifying your income streams is essential for building wealth and achieving financial success. By exploring passive income opportunities, taking on side hustles, and investing in the stock market, you can create multiple sources of revenue that can support you in times of need and help you continue to grow your wealth over time. Remember, the key to financial stability and success is not just to rely on one source of income, but to build a diverse portfolio of income streams that can sustain you for the long term.

Leveraging Passive Income Opportunities

Passive income is a key component of wealth building that allows you to earn money without actively working for it. In this subchapter, we will explore the various passive income opportunities available to everyone seeking to build their wealth. By leveraging these opportunities, you can create additional streams of income that will help you achieve financial freedom and security.

One of the most popular passive income opportunities is real estate investing. By purchasing rental properties, you can generate a steady stream of income from tenants while also building equity in the property itself. This form of passive income requires an initial investment, but it can be a lucrative long-term strategy for wealth building.

Another passive income opportunity is investing in dividend-paying stocks. By purchasing shares of companies that pay dividends to their shareholders, you can earn regular income without having to actively manage the investment. This can be a great way to build wealth over time, especially if you reinvest the dividends to purchase more shares.

Creating and selling digital products is another passive income opportunity that has become increasingly popular in the digital age. By creating e-books, online courses, or digital downloads, you can generate income from sales without having to continuously produce new content. This can be a great way to leverage your expertise and earn passive income while helping others learn and grow.

Finally, affiliate marketing is a passive income opportunity that involves promoting products or services from other companies and earning a commission on sales. By partnering with companies that offer affiliate programs, you can earn a passive income stream by driving traffic and sales to their products. This can be a great way to monetize your website, blog, or social media presence and generate income while you sleep.

In conclusion, leveraging passive income opportunities is a powerful strategy for wealth building that can help you achieve financial success. By diversifying your income streams and investing in opportunities that align with your skills and interests, you can build a solid foundation for long-term wealth and security. Take advantage of these passive income opportunities and start building the wealth you deserve today.

Negotiating Salary and Benefits

Negotiating salary and benefits is a crucial step in building wealth and securing financial stability. Whether you are just starting out in your career or looking to make a move to a new company, it is important to advocate for yourself and ensure you are being properly compensated for your skills and experience. This subchapter will provide you with valuable tips and strategies for negotiating salary and benefits effectively.

When negotiating your salary, it is essential to do your research and know your worth. Research typical salaries for your position and industry. Take into account factors such as location, experience, and education. This information will give you leverage when discussing compensation with potential employers. Remember, you are not just negotiating for your current salary, but also setting the stage for future raises and bonuses.

In addition to salary, benefits are an important part of your overall compensation package. Be sure to consider factors such as health insurance, retirement savings plans, paid time off, and other perks when evaluating a job offer. These benefits can have a significant impact on your financial well-being and should not be overlooked during negotiations. Remember, it is okay to ask for more or negotiate different benefits if the initial offer does not meet your needs.

During negotiations, be confident and assertive making sure to advocate for yourself. Clearly communicate your value to the company and provide examples of your skills and accomplishments. Be prepared to discuss what sets you apart from other candidates and how you can contribute to the company's success. Remember, negotiating is a two-way street, and it is important to listen carefully to the employer's needs and concerns as well.

Lastly, be prepared to walk away if the employer is not willing to meet your salary and benefit requirements. It is better to hold out for a job offer that meets your financial needs and aligns with your long-term goals than to accept a subpar offer out of desperation. Remember, you have worked hard to build your skills and experience, and you deserve to be compensated fairly for your

Wealth Building Secrets: Strategies for Success for Everyone

contributions. By negotiating salary and benefits effectively, you can set yourself up for long-term financial success and build wealth for the future.

Chapter 4: Investment Principles for Wealth Building

Understanding Risk Tolerance

Understanding your risk tolerance is a crucial aspect of wealth building. Risk tolerance refers to the amount of uncertainty or volatility you are willing to endure when making investment decisions. It is important to assess your risk tolerance before making any financial decisions, as it can greatly impact the success of your wealth-building strategy. By understanding your risk tolerance, you can make informed decisions that align with your financial goals and objectives.

There are several factors that can influence your risk tolerance, including your age, financial goals, investment experience, and personal preferences. Younger individuals typically have a higher risk tolerance, as they have more time to recover from any potential losses. On the other hand, older individuals may have a lower risk tolerance, as they may be closer to retirement and have less time to recover from any financial setbacks. It is important to take all of these factors into consideration when assessing your risk tolerance.

It is important to remember that risk tolerance is not a one-size-fits-all concept. What works for one person may not work for another. It is important to take the time to evaluate your own risk tolerance and determine what level of risk you are comfortable with. This can help you make more informed decisions when it comes to investing and wealth building.

One way to assess your risk tolerance is to take a risk tolerance questionnaire. These questionnaires are designed to help you understand your comfort level with different types of investments and the level of risk you are willing to take on. By answering a series of questions about your financial goals, investment experience, and personal preferences, you can get a better understanding of your risk tolerance and make more informed decisions.

In conclusion, understanding your risk tolerance is essential for successful wealth building. By assessing your risk tolerance and aligning your investment decisions with your comfort level, you can create a financial strategy that is tailored to your individual needs and goals. Take the time to evaluate your risk tolerance and make informed decisions that will help you achieve financial success in the long run.

Asset Allocation Strategies

Asset allocation is a crucial component of any successful wealth-building strategy. By strategically allocating your assets across a diversified portfolio, you can minimize risk and maximize returns. There are several asset allocation strategies that you can implement to achieve your financial goals.

One popular asset allocation strategy is the "age-based" approach. This strategy involves adjusting the allocation of your assets based on your age and risk tolerance. For example, when you are younger, you may have a higher risk tolerance and can afford to invest more heavily in stocks. As you get older and approach retirement, you may want to shift towards more conservative investments, such as bonds and cash.

Another asset allocation strategy is the "risk-based" approach. This strategy involves assessing your risk tolerance and investing in assets that align with your risk profile. If you are more risk-averse, you may choose to allocate a larger portion of your portfolio to safer investments, such as bonds and cash. If you are comfortable with taking on more risk, you may opt for a more aggressive allocation with a higher exposure to stocks.

A third asset allocation strategy is the "goal-based" approach. This strategy involves aligning your asset allocation with specific financial goals, such as saving for retirement, buying a home, or funding your children's education. By tailoring your asset allocation to your individual goals, you can ensure that your investments are working towards achieving the outcomes you desire.

Regardless of which asset allocation strategy you choose, it is important to regularly review and adjust your portfolio to ensure that it remains aligned with your financial goals and risk tolerance. By diversifying your assets and implementing a thoughtful asset allocation strategy, you can build wealth over time and achieve financial success.

Real Estate Investing

Real estate investing is one of the most popular ways to build wealth and create financial stability for the long term. Whether you are a seasoned investor or just starting out, there are key strategies and secrets that can help you succeed in the real estate market. In this subchapter, we will explore the fundamentals of real estate investing and provide valuable insights for those looking to grow their wealth through property ownership.

One of the first things to consider when getting into real estate investing is your financial goals and risk tolerance.

Wealth Building Secrets: Strategies for Success for Everyone

Are you looking to generate passive income through rental properties, or do you want to flip houses for quick profits? Understanding your objectives will help you determine the best investment strategy for your situation. Additionally, it is important to assess your risk tolerance and establish a comfortable level of exposure to the real estate market.

Another key aspect of successful real estate investing is conducting thorough research and due diligence. This includes analyzing market trends, property values, and potential rental income in the area you are considering investing in. By gathering as much information as possible, you can make informed decisions that will increase your chances of success in the real estate market.

When it comes to actually purchasing a property, it is essential to carefully consider your financing options. Whether you choose to finance your investment through a traditional mortgage, private lender, or cash purchase, it is crucial to weigh the pros and cons of each method and select the option that aligns with your financial goals and risk tolerance. Additionally, working with a knowledgeable real estate agent or investment advisor can help you navigate the complexities of property transactions and ensure a smooth process.

In conclusion, real estate investing can be a lucrative and rewarding way to build wealth for the long term. By understanding your financial goals, conducting thorough research, and carefully considering your financing options, you can set yourself up for success in the real estate market. Whether you are a seasoned investor or just starting out, the strategies and secrets outlined in this subchapter can help you achieve your wealth-building goals through property ownership.

Chapter 5: Advanced Wealth Building Techniques

Tax Planning Strategies

Tax planning strategies are essential for building and preserving wealth for everyone. By strategically managing your taxes, you can maximize your savings and investments, ultimately increasing your overall wealth. In this subchapter, we will explore some key tax planning strategies that can help you achieve financial success.

One effective tax planning strategy is to take advantage of tax-deferred accounts, such as 401(k) plans or individual retirement accounts (IRAs). By contributing to these accounts, you can reduce your taxable income and save for retirement at the same time. Additionally, many employers offer matching contributions to 401(k) plans, which can further boost your savings. By utilizing tax-deferred accounts, you can lower your current tax liability and grow your wealth over time.

Another important tax planning strategy is to carefully consider the timing of your income and expenses. By strategically timing when you receive income and incur expenses, you can minimize your tax liability. For example: If you have the flexibility to delay receiving a bonus or selling an investment until the following year, you can push your tax liability into the future. Similarly, by accelerating deductible expenses, such as charitable contributions or mortgage interest payments, you can reduce your taxable income in the current year.

One often overlooked tax planning strategy is taking advantage of tax credits and deductions. Tax credits directly reduce your tax liability, while deductions lower your taxable income. By maximizing these opportunities, you can significantly reduce the amount of taxes you owe. For example, you may be eligible for tax credits for education expenses, energy-efficient home improvements, or child care expenses. Additionally, deductions for medical expenses, mortgage interest, and charitable contributions can further lower your tax bill.

Lastly, it is important to regularly review and update your tax planning strategy to ensure that it aligns with your financial goals. Tax laws and regulations are constantly changing, so it is essential to stay informed and adapt your strategy accordingly. By working with a qualified tax professional, you can develop a personalized tax plan that maximizes your savings and helps you achieve your wealth-building goals. Remember, proactive tax planning is key to building and preserving wealth for everyone.

Estate Planning

Estate planning is a crucial aspect of wealth building that is often overlooked by many individuals. It involves making decisions about how your assets will be distributed after your passing, ensuring that your loved ones are taken care of and your legacy is preserved. By creating a comprehensive estate plan, you can minimize taxes, avoid probate, and protect your assets from creditors.

One of the key components of estate planning is creating

a will. A will is a legal document that outlines how you want your assets to be distributed upon your death. Without a will, your assets may be distributed according to state laws, which may not align with your wishes. By creating a will, you can ensure that your assets are distributed according to your wishes and that your loved ones are taken care of.

Another important aspect of estate planning is establishing a trust. A trust is a legal entity that holds assets on behalf of a beneficiary. By setting up a trust, you can avoid probate, minimize taxes, and provide for the ongoing management of your assets. Trusts can also be used to protect assets from creditors and ensure that your assets are distributed according to your wishes.

In addition to creating a will and establishing a trust, estate planning also involves designating beneficiaries for your retirement accounts, life insurance policies, and other assets. By designating beneficiaries, you can ensure that these assets are transferred directly to your loved ones without going through probate. This can help

to expedite the distribution of your assets and minimize taxes.

Overall, estate planning is a critical component of wealth building that should not be overlooked. By creating a comprehensive estate plan, you can ensure that your assets are distributed according to your wishes, minimize taxes, and protect your loved ones. Whether you are just starting to build your wealth or have already accumulated significant assets, estate planning is a key step in securing your financial legacy for future generations.

Leveraging Financial Advisors

In the world of wealth building, one of the most valuable resources you can have at your disposal is a financial advisor. These professionals are trained to help you navigate the complex world of investments, savings, and financial planning. By leveraging the expertise of a financial advisor, you can make informed decisions that

Wealth Building Secrets: Strategies for Success for Everyone

will help you build and protect your wealth over the long term.

One of the key benefits of working with a financial advisor is their ability to help you create a comprehensive financial plan. This plan will outline your financial goals, as well as the strategies you will use to achieve them. By working with a financial advisor to create a plan tailored to your specific needs and objectives, you can ensure that you are on the right track to building wealth and securing your financial future.

Another advantage of working with a financial advisor is their ability to provide you with expert advice and guidance on a wide range of financial topics. Whether you are looking to invest in the stock market, save for retirement, or plan for your children's education, a financial advisor can help you make smart decisions that will maximize your financial potential. By leveraging the knowledge and expertise of a financial advisor, you can avoid common pitfalls and make informed choices that will benefit you in the long run.

In addition to providing you with expert advice and guidance, a financial advisor can also help you stay on track with your financial goals. By regularly reviewing your financial plan and making adjustments as needed, your financial advisor can help you adapt to changes in your financial situation and ensure that you are always working towards your goals. This ongoing support and accountability can be invaluable in helping you build wealth and achieve financial success.

Ultimately, by leveraging the expertise and support of a financial advisor, you can take control of your financial future and build wealth with confidence. Whether you are just starting out on your wealth-building journey or looking to take your financial success to the next level, working with a financial advisor can help you achieve your goals and secure your financial future. Don't hesitate to reach out to a financial advisor today and start taking steps towards building the wealth you deserve.

Chapter 6: Maintaining and Growing Wealth

Revisiting and Adjusting Financial Goals

Revisiting and adjusting financial goals is a crucial step in the wealth-building journey. As circumstances and priorities change, it is important to reassess and realign your financial goals to ensure you are on track to achieve the success you desire. Whether you are just starting out on your wealth-building journey or have been working towards your goals for some time, taking the time to revisit and adjust your financial goals can help you stay focused and motivated.

One of the first steps in revisiting and adjusting financial goals is to take stock of your current financial situation. This includes looking at your income, expenses, assets, and debts. By understanding where you stand financially, you can better assess what adjustments may be necessary to reach your goals. This may involve cutting expenses, increasing income, or reallocating resources to better align with your objectives.

Once you have a clear picture of your current financial situation, it is important to revisit your long-term financial goals. Are they still relevant and attainable? Have any circumstances changed that may impact your ability to achieve these goals? By asking these questions and reassessing your goals, you can make any necessary adjustments to ensure they remain achievable and in line with your overall financial plan.

Adjusting financial goals may also involve setting new targets or milestones to help keep you motivated and on track. These could be short-term goals that can help you stay focused and track your progress towards your larger objectives. By breaking down your goals into smaller, achievable steps, you can maintain momentum and celebrate your successes along the way.

In conclusion, revisiting and adjusting financial goals is a key part of the wealth- building process. By regularly reassessing your goals, taking stock of your financial situation, and making necessary adjustments, you can stay on track towards achieving the success you desire. Remember, financial goals are not set in stone and can evolve over time as circumstances change. Stay flexible, stay focused, and keep working towards your dreams of financial independence and wealth-building success.

Monitoring and Tracking Financial Progress

Monitoring and tracking your financial progress is essential when it comes to building wealth. Without keeping a close eye on your finances, it can be easy to lose track of where your money is going and how it is growing. In this subchapter, we will discuss the importance of monitoring and tracking your financial progress, as well as provide some tips and strategies to help you stay on top of your finances.

One of the first steps in monitoring your financial progress is to create a budget. A budget is a valuable tool that can help you track your income and expenses, as well as identify areas where you may be overspending. By creating a budget and sticking to it, you can ensure that you are living within your means and saving money for the future.

In addition to creating a budget, it is important to track your spending regularly. This can be done through various methods, such as using a budgeting app or keeping a spending journal. By tracking your spending, you can identify any areas where you may be overspending and make adjustments as needed to stay on track with your financial goals.

Another important aspect of monitoring your financial progress is regularly reviewing your investments and savings accounts. By keeping a close eye on your investment portfolio and savings accounts, you can ensure that your money is growing at a steady rate and that you are on track to meet your financial goals. If necessary, you can make adjustments to your investments to ensure that they are aligned with your long-term financial objectives.

In conclusion, monitoring and tracking your financial progress is crucial when it comes to building wealth. By creating a budget, tracking your spending, and regularly reviewing your investments and savings accounts, you can ensure that you are on the right path to financial success. Remember, building wealth is a journey that requires dedication and discipline, but with the right strategies in place, anyone can achieve financial prosperity.

Giving Back and Philanthropy

Giving back and philanthropy are essential components of wealth building that often go overlooked. Many people think that building wealth is solely about accumulating money and assets, but true wealth also comes from giving back to those in need. Philanthropy is not just for the ultra-rich; everyone can make a difference, no matter how big or small.

One of the key principles of wealth building is the concept of abundance. By giving back to others, you are demonstrating your belief in abundance and attracting more wealth into your life. When you give freely and generously, you are sending a powerful message to the universe that you are open to receiving even more in return. This cycle of giving and receiving is a fundamental principle of wealth building that can lead to greater success and fulfillment in all areas of your life.

Philanthropy is also a way to create a lasting legacy and impact future generations. By giving back to causes that are important to you, you are leaving a positive mark on the world and making a difference in the lives of others. Whether you choose to donate money, time, or resources, your philanthropic efforts can have a ripple effect that extends far beyond your own lifetime.

In addition to the personal benefits of giving back, philanthropy can also have a positive impact on your wealth building efforts. By supporting causes that align with your values and goals, you are creating a sense of purpose and fulfillment that can motivate you to work harder and achieve greater success. Giving back can also help you build valuable connections and relationships with like-minded individuals who share your passion for making a difference in the world.

In conclusion, giving back and philanthropy are essential components of wealth building that can lead to greater success, fulfillment, and impact. Whether you choose to donate money, time, or resources, your philanthropic efforts can have a positive effect on your own life as well as the lives of others. By embracing the principles of abundance and generosity, you can attract more wealth into your life and create a lasting legacy that will benefit future generations. Remember, true wealth is not just about what you have; it's also about what you give.

Chapter 7: Overcoming Common Wealth Building Challenges

Dealing with Setbacks and Failures

In the world of wealth building, setbacks and failures are inevitable. No matter how well you plan or how hard you work, there will always be obstacles that stand in your way. However, it's important to remember that setbacks are not the end of the road - they are simply opportunities for growth and learning. In this subchapter, we will discuss how to deal with setbacks and failures in a positive and productive way.

The first step in dealing with setbacks and failures is to accept them as a natural part of the wealth building journey. Instead of viewing them as insurmountable obstacles, see them as opportunities to reassess your goals and strategies. By acknowledging and accepting your setbacks, you can begin to move forward with a clear mind and a renewed sense of determination.

Wealth Building Secrets: Strategies for Success for Everyone

One of the most important things to remember when facing setbacks is to stay positive. It can be easy to get discouraged when things don't go as planned, but maintaining a positive attitude is crucial to overcoming obstacles. Remember that setbacks are temporary and that you have the power to turn things around. By staying positive and focused on your goals, you can overcome any setback that comes your way.

Another key strategy for dealing with setbacks and failures is to learn from them. Take the time to reflect on what went wrong and why, and use this knowledge to improve your strategies moving forward. By analyzing your failures and learning from them, you can avoid making the same mistakes in the future and increase your chances of success.

In conclusion, setbacks and failures are a natural part of the wealth building journey. By accepting them, staying positive, and learning from them, you can overcome any obstacle that comes your way. Remember that setbacks are not the end of the road - they are simply opportunities for growth and improvement. Stay focused on your goals, and you will ultimately achieve success in your wealth building endeavors.

Overcoming Impulse Spending

Impulse spending is a common obstacle that many people face when trying to build wealth. It can be tempting to make spur-of-the-moment purchases, especially when we see something we want or feel like we deserve a treat.

However, giving in to these impulses can quickly derail our financial goals. In this subchapter, we will explore strategies for overcoming impulse spending and staying on track towards building wealth.

The first step in overcoming impulse spending is to identify your triggers. Take some time to reflect on what situations or emotions tend to lead you to make impulsive purchases. Maybe you shop when you're stressed, bored, or feeling down. By understanding your triggers, you can develop strategies to avoid them or find healthier ways to cope. This self-awareness is key to breaking the cycle of impulse spending.

Another effective strategy for overcoming impulse spending is to create a budget and stick to it. Having a clear plan for how you will allocate your money can help you resist the temptation to make unnecessary purchases. Make sure to include a category for discretionary spending in your budget, but set limits for yourself and prioritize your financial goals. This will help you make more intentional choices about how you use your money.

One helpful technique for curbing impulse spending is to implement a "cooling off" period before making any non-essential purchases. This could be as simple as waiting 24 hours before buying something you want. During this time, ask yourself if the purchase aligns with your financial goals and if you truly need or value the item. Often, you will find that the impulse to buy fades away, saving you money in the long run.

Finally, surround yourself with a supportive community that shares your wealth- building goals. Having friends, family, or mentors who understand your financial aspirations can provide encouragement and accountability when it comes to managing your spending habits. Share your successes and challenges with them, and lean on their guidance when you feel tempted to give in to impulse spending. Remember, building wealth is a journey that requires discipline and commitment, but with the right strategies and support, you can overcome impulse spending and achieve your financial goals.

Handling Family and Relationship Dynamics

In the journey to building wealth, it is important to consider the impact that family and relationship dynamics can have on your financial success. Family members, whether they are supportive or not, can greatly influence your mindset, beliefs, and behaviors around money. It is essential to navigate these relationships with care and awareness in order to maintain a healthy balance between personal goals and familial expectations.

One key aspect of handling family dynamics is setting boundaries. It is important to communicate openly with your loved ones about your financial goals and priorities. Setting boundaries can help prevent conflicts and misunderstandings, ensuring that everyone is on the same page when it comes to money matters. Remember that it is okay to say no to financial requests that do not align with your goals, as ultimately, you are responsible for your own financial well-being.

Another important aspect of managing family dynamics is identifying and addressing any underlying beliefs or patterns that may be impacting your relationship with money. Take the time to reflect on how your family's attitudes towards money have influenced your own views and behaviors. By identifying and addressing these beliefs, you can begin to shift your mindset towards one that is more conducive to building wealth and achieving financial success.

Wealth Building Secrets: Strategies for Success for Everyone

When it comes to relationships, it is essential to choose partners and friends who support your financial goals and aspirations. Surround yourself with individuals who share similar values and beliefs around money, as this can help reinforce positive financial habits and behaviors. Additionally, communication is key in any relationship, so be sure to have open and honest conversations about money with your partner to ensure that you are both working towards the same financial goals.

In conclusion, navigating family and relationship dynamics is a crucial aspect of building wealth. By setting boundaries, addressing underlying beliefs, and surrounding yourself with supportive individuals, you can create a positive environment that fosters financial success. Remember that you are in control of your own financial future, and by taking proactive steps to manage your relationships, you can set yourself up for long-term prosperity and abundance.

Chapter 8: Wealth Building for Everyone

Strategies for Individuals with Low Income

In the subchapter "Strategies for Individuals with Low Income" in the book "Wealth Building Secrets: Strategies for Success for Everyone," we will explore practical tips and techniques for those facing financial challenges. It is important to remember that wealth building is possible for everyone, regardless of their current income level. By implementing the right strategies and making smart financial choices, individuals with low income can start on the path towards financial success.

One of the key strategies for individuals with low income is to create a budget and stick to it. By tracking expenses and identifying areas where money can be saved, individuals can better manage their finances and allocate funds towards savings and investments. It is important to prioritize essential expenses such as housing, utilities, and food, while cutting back on non-essential items. By living within their means and avoiding unnecessary expenses, individuals can start building wealth even with a limited income.

Another important strategy for individuals with low income is to increase their earning potential. This can be achieved through education and training, seeking higher paying job opportunities, or starting a side business. By investing in their skills and expertise, individuals can increase their income and create additional sources of revenue. It is important to be proactive and take steps towards improving one's financial situation, rather than relying solely on a fixed income.

Additionally, individuals with low income can benefit from seeking out financial assistance and resources available to them. This may include government programs, nonprofit organizations, or community services that provide support for individuals facing financial challenges. By taking advantage of these resources, individuals can access valuable tools and information to help them improve their financial situation and build wealth over time.

Overall, the key to success for individuals with low income is to be proactive, disciplined, and focused on their financial goals. By implementing strategies such as budgeting, increasing earning potential, and seeking out resources, individuals can overcome financial obstacles and achieve long-term financial stability. Wealth building is possible for everyone, and with the right mindset and determination, individuals can create a brighter financial future for themselves and their families.

Wealth Building for Entrepreneurs

Wealth building is a crucial aspect of entrepreneurship that can help individuals achieve financial freedom and success. In this subchapter, we will explore key strategies for entrepreneurs to build wealth and secure their financial future. By implementing these strategies, entrepreneurs can maximize their earning potential and create a solid foundation for long-term wealth accumulation.

Wealth Building Secrets: Strategies for Success for Everyone

One of the most important wealth-building strategies for entrepreneurs is to invest in themselves and their businesses. This can involve acquiring new skills, expanding their knowledge, and taking calculated risks to grow their ventures. By continuously improving themselves and their businesses, entrepreneurs can increase their earning potential and create more opportunities for wealth accumulation.

Another key strategy for wealth building for entrepreneurs is to diversify their income streams. Relying solely on one source of income can be risky, as it leaves entrepreneurs vulnerable to economic downturns and industry disruptions. By diversifying their income streams through multiple revenue sources, such as investments, side businesses, and passive income streams, entrepreneurs can create a more stable financial foundation and increase their overall wealth.

In addition to investing in themselves and diversifying

their income streams, entrepreneurs should also prioritize saving and investing a portion of their earnings. By setting aside a portion of their income for savings and investments, entrepreneurs can build a safety net for unexpected expenses and create opportunities for their money to grow over time. This disciplined approach to saving and investing can help entrepreneurs achieve their long-term wealth- building goals.

Overall, wealth building for entrepreneurs requires a combination of strategic planning, continuous learning, and disciplined financial management. By investing in themselves, diversifying their income streams, and prioritizing saving and investing, entrepreneurs can create a solid foundation for long-term wealth accumulation and financial success. With dedication and perseverance, entrepreneurs can achieve their wealth-building goals and secure their financial future.

Wealth Building for Young Adults

Building wealth is a goal that many young adults aspire to

Wealth Building Secrets: Strategies for Success for Everyone

achieve, but it can often seem like an overwhelming task. However, with the right strategies and mindset, young adults can set themselves up for financial success in the long run. In this subchapter, we will explore some key wealth-building tips specifically tailored for young adults looking to secure their financial future.

One of the most important things young adults can do to start building wealth is to establish a budget and stick to it. By tracking their expenses and income, young adults can gain a better understanding of where their money is going and identify areas where they can cut back on unnecessary spending. This disciplined approach to money management is crucial for laying the foundation for long-term financial success.

Another key wealth-building strategy for young adults is to start investing early. By taking advantage of compound interest and the power of time, young adults can significantly grow their wealth over the years. Whether it's through a retirement account, stocks, or real estate, investing early and consistently can help young adults build a solid financial foundation for the future.

In addition to budgeting and investing, young adults should also focus on increasing their income potential. This can be done through furthering their education, acquiring new skills, or pursuing entrepreneurship opportunities. By increasing their earning potential, young adults can accelerate their wealth- building journey and achieve their financial goals faster.

Lastly, young adults should prioritize saving for emergencies and unexpected expenses. Having a financial safety net in place can provide peace of mind and prevent young adults from going into debt when faced with unforeseen circumstances. By building up an emergency fund, young adults can protect their financial well-being and stay on track with their wealth-building goals.

In conclusion, wealth-building for young adults is a journey that requires discipline, patience, and strategic planning.

Wealth Building Secrets: Strategies for Success for Everyone

By establishing a budget, investing early, increasing income potential, and saving for emergencies, young adults can set themselves up for financial success in the long run. With the right mindset and dedication, young adults can achieve their wealth-building goals and secure a prosperous future for themselves.

Chapter 9: Conclusion

Recap of Key Wealth Building Principles

In this subchapter, we will recap some of the key wealth building principles discussed throughout this book. These principles are essential for anyone looking to improve their financial situation and build long-term wealth. By understanding and applying these principles, you can set yourself on the path to financial success.

The first key wealth building principle is the importance of setting clear financial goals. Without specific goals in mind, it can be difficult to stay motivated and focused on building wealth. By setting goals for saving, investing, and increasing your income, you can create a roadmap for achieving financial success.

Wealth Building Secrets: Strategies for Success for Everyone

Another important principle is the power of compounding. By starting to save and invest early, you can take advantage of the power of compounding to grow your wealth over time. Even small contributions can add up significantly over the long term, so it's important to start building your wealth as soon as possible.

Diversification is also a key wealth building principle. By spreading your investments across different asset classes, industries, and geographic regions, you can reduce your overall risk and increase your chances of achieving long-term financial success. Diversification is an important strategy for managing risk and maximizing returns in your investment portfolio.

Finally, the principle of continuous learning is crucial for building wealth. The financial markets are constantly changing, so it's important to stay informed and educated about the latest trends and developments. By continuously learning and adapting your financial strategies, you can position yourself for success in any economic environment. By applying these key wealth building principles, you can improve your financial situation and build long-term wealth for yourself and your family.

Tips for Continued Success

In the world of wealth building, success is not a one-time achievement. It requires consistent effort, dedication, and a willingness to adapt to changing circumstances. To help you on your journey to continued success, here are some essential tips to keep in mind:

1. Set clear goals and create a solid plan: Without a clear vision of what you want to achieve and a plan to get there, it's easy to lose focus and get off track. Take the time to set specific, measurable goals for your wealth building journey and create a detailed plan outlining the steps you need to take to reach them. This will help you stay motivated and on course, even when faced with challenges.

Wealth Building Secrets: Strategies for Success for Everyone

2. Stay informed and educated: The world of wealth building is constantly evolving, with new opportunities and risks emerging all the time. To stay ahead of the game, it's essential to stay informed and educated about the latest trends, strategies, and tools available to help you grow your wealth. Take the time to read books, attend seminars, and seek out advice from experts in the field to keep your knowledge and skills sharp.

3. Diversify your investments: One of the keys to long-term success in wealth building is diversification. By spreading your investments across different asset classes, industries, and geographic regions, you can reduce your risk exposure and increase your chances of success. Make sure to regularly review and adjust your investment portfolio to ensure it remains well-diversified and aligned with your financial goals.

4. Practice patience and discipline: Building wealth takes time and requires a great deal of patience and discipline. Don't expect to see instant results or get discouraged by

setbacks along the way. Stay focused on your long-term goals, stick to your plan, and be willing to make tough decisions when necessary. By practicing patience and discipline, you'll be better equipped to weather the ups and downs of the wealth building journey.

5. Seek out mentors and build a support network: Success in wealth building is not a solo endeavor. Surround yourself with like-minded individuals who share your goals and values, and seek out mentors who can offer guidance, advice, and support along the way. Building a strong support network will not only help you stay motivated and accountable but also provide valuable insights and perspectives to help you navigate the challenges of wealth building more effectively.

By following these essential tips for continued success in wealth building, you'll be better equipped to achieve your financial goals and create a secure and prosperous future for yourself and your loved ones. Remember, wealth building is a journey, not a destination, so stay committed, stay focused, and keep pushing forward towards your dreams.

Resources for Further Learning

Congratulations on taking the first step towards building your wealth! As you continue on your journey to financial success, it's important to continuously educate yourself on the best strategies and techniques for wealth building. Here are some resources that can help you further your learning and achieve your financial goals:

1. Books: There are countless books available on wealth building, personal finance, and investing that can provide valuable insights and knowledge. Some recommended titles include "Rich Dad Poor Dad" by Robert Kiyosaki, "The Millionaire Next Door" by Thomas J. Stanley, and "The Intelligent Investor" by Benjamin Graham. These books offer practical advice and strategies for building wealth and achieving financial independence.

2. Online Courses: The internet is a treasure trove of resources for learning about wealth building. There are numerous online courses and programs available that cover a wide range of topics, such as investing, budgeting, and entrepreneurship. Websites like Coursera, Udemy, and Khan Academy offer courses taught by experts in the field that can help you deepen your understanding of wealth building principles.

3. Podcasts: If you prefer to learn on-the-go, podcasts can be a great way to absorb information about wealth building. There are many podcasts hosted by financial experts and entrepreneurs that cover topics such as investing, real estate, and personal finance. Some popular podcasts in this genre include "The Dave Ramsey Show," "The Tim Ferriss Show," and "Afford Anything."

4. Financial Advisors: If you're looking for personalized guidance and advice on wealth building, consider working with a financial advisor. A professional advisor can help

Wealth Building Secrets: Strategies for Success for Everyone

you create a customized financial plan tailored to your goals and circumstances. They can also provide ongoing support and guidance as you work towards building your wealth.

5. Networking Events: Building relationships with like-minded individuals can be a valuable resource for further learning about wealth building. Attending networking events, seminars, and workshops can help you connect with other individuals who share your goals and aspirations. You can learn from their experiences, exchange ideas, and gain valuable insights that can help you on your wealth building journey.

By taking advantage of these resources for further learning, you can continue to expand your knowledge and expertise in wealth building. Remember, building wealth is a journey that requires continuous education, dedication, and hard work. With the right tools and resources at your disposal, you can achieve your financial goals and create a secure future for yourself and your loved ones.

www.ingramcontent.com/pod-product-compliance
Lightning Source LLC
Chambersburg PA
CBHW050237230526
45470CB00005B/1994